2nd Workshop on Semantic Interpretation in an Actionable Context 2012

Held at the 2012 Conference of the North American Chapter of the Association for Computational Linguistics: Human Language Technologies (NAACL-HLT 2012)

Montreal, Quebec, Canada
3 – 8 June 2012

ISBN: 978-1-62276-574-4

Printed from e-media with permission by:

Curran Associates, Inc.
57 Morehouse Lane
Red Hook, NY 12571

CURRAN ASSOCIATES INC. proceedings.com

Some format issues inherent in the e-media version may also appear in this print version.

Printed by Curran Associates, Inc. (2013)

For permission requests, please contact the Association for Computational Linguistics at the address below.

Association for Computational Linguistics
209 N. Eighth Street
Stroudsburg, Pennsylvania 18360

Phone: 1-570-476-8006
Fax: 1-570-476-0860

acl@aclweb.org

Additional copies of this publication are available from:

Curran Associates, Inc.
57 Morehouse Lane
Red Hook, NY 12571 USA
Phone: 845-758-0400
Fax: 845-758-2634
Email: curran@proceedings.com
Web: www.proceedings.com

Introduction

Effective and seamless Human-Computer interaction using natural language is arguably one of the major challenges of natural language processing and artificial intelligence in general. Making significant progress in developing natural language capabilities that support this level of interaction has countless applications and is bound to attract many researchers from several AI fields: from robotics to games to the social sciences.

From the natural language processing perspective the problem is often formulated as a translation task: mapping between natural language input and a logical output language that can be executed in the domain of interest. Unlike shallow approaches for semantic interpretation, which provide an incomplete or underspecified interpretation of the natural language input, the output of a formal semantic interpreter is expected to provide complete meaning representation that can be executed directly by a computer system. Examples of such systems include robotic control, database access, game playing and more.

Current approaches to this task take a data driven approach, in which a learning algorithm is given a set of natural language sentences as input and their corresponding logical meaning representation and learns a statistical semantic parser: a set of parameterized rules mapping lexical items and syntactic patterns to a logical formula.

In recent years this framework was challenged by an exciting line of research, advocating that semantic interpretation should not be studied in isolation, but rather in the context of the external environment (or computer system) which provides the semantic context for interpretation. This line of research comprises several directions, focusing on grounded semantic representations, flexible semantic interpretation models, and alternative learning protocols driven by indirect supervision signals. This progress has contributed to expanding the scope of semantic interpretation, introduced new domains and tasks and revealed that it is possible to make progress in this direction with reduced manual effort. In particular, it resulted in a wide range of models, learning protocols, learning tasks, and semantic formalisms that, while clearly related, are not directly comparable and understood under a single framework.

The workshop consists mostly of invited speakers, but will also include several novel works. The goal of this workshop is to provide researchers interested in the field with an opportunity to exchange ideas, discuss other perspectives, and formulate a shared vision for this research direction.

Organizers:

Dan Goldwasser, University of Illinois at Urbana Champaign (USA)
Regina Barzilay, Massachusetts Institute of Technology (USA)
Dan Roth, University of Illinois at Urbana Champaign (USA)

Program Committee:

Raymond Mooney, University of Texas at Austin (USA)
Luke Zettlemoyer, University of Washington (USA)
Jacob Eisenstein, Georgia Tech (USA)
Alexander Koller, University of Potsdam (Germany)
Percy Liang, Google (USA)
Wei Lu, University of Illinois at Urbana Champaign (USA)
Nick Roy, Massachusetts Institute of Technology (USA)
Jeffrey Mark Siskind, Purdue University (USA)
Jason Weston, Google (USA)

Additional Reviewers:

Rajhans Samdani, University of Illinois at Urbana Champaign (USA)

Invited Speaker:

Raymond Mooney, University of Texas at Austin (USA)
Luke Zettlemoyer, University of Washington (USA)
Yoshua Bengio, University of Montréal (Canada)
Julia Hockenmaier, University of Illinois at Urbana Champaign (USA)
Dan Roth, University of Illinois at Urbana Champaign (USA)
Mehdi Hafezi Manshadi, University of Rochester (USA)

Table of Contents

Conference Program

June 8

9:00 **Morning Session**

Workshop Introduction
Workshop organizers

Learning to Interpret Natural Language Instructions
Monica Babes-Vroman, James MacGlashan, Ruoyuan Gao, Kevin Winner, Richard Adjogah, Marie desJardins, Michael Littman and Smaranda Muresan

Toward Learning Perceptually Grounded Word Meanings from Unaligned Parallel Data
Stefanie Tellex, Pratiksha Thaker, Josh Joseph, and Nicholas Roy

Invited Talk: Integrating Natural Language Programming and Programming by Demonstration
Mehdi Hafezi Manshadi

10:30 **Coffee Break**

11:00 **Morning Session 2**

Invited Talk: Learning to Interpret Natural Language Navigation Instructions from Observation
Raymond Mooney

12:00 **Lunch**

13:00 **Afternoon Session**

Invited Talk:
Luke Zettlemoyer

Invited Talk:
Yoshua Bengio

15:00 **Coffee Break**

15:30 **Afternoon Session 2**

Invited Talk:
Julia Hockenmaier

Invited Talk:
Dan Roth

Learning to Interpret Natural Language Instructions

Monica Babeş-Vroman[+], **James MacGlashan**[*], **Ruoyuan Gao**[+], **Kevin Winner**[*]
Richard Adjogah[*], **Marie desJardins**[*], **Michael Littman**[+] and **Smaranda Muresan**[++]

[*] Department of Computer Science and Electrical Engineering
University of Maryland, Baltimore County
[+] Computer Science Department, Rutgers University
[++] School of Communication and Information, Rutgers University

Abstract

This paper addresses the problem of training an artificial agent to follow verbal instructions representing high-level tasks using a set of instructions paired with demonstration traces of appropriate behavior. From this data, a mapping from instructions to tasks is learned, enabling the agent to carry out new instructions in novel environments.

1 Introduction

Learning to interpret language from a situated context has become a topic of much interest in recent years (Branavan et al., 2009; Branavan et al., 2010; Branavan et al., 2011; Clarke et al., 2010; Chen and Mooney, 2011; Vogel and Jurafsky, 2010; Goldwasser and Roth, 2011; Liang et al., 2011; Atrzi and Zettlemoyer, 2011; Tellex et al., 2011). Instead of using annotated training data consisting of sentences and their corresponding logical forms (Zettlemoyer and Collins, 2005; Kate and Mooney, 2006; Wong and Mooney, 2007; Zettlemoyer and Collins, 2009; Lu et al., 2008), most of these approaches leverage non-linguistic information from a situated context as their primary source of supervision. These approaches have been applied to various tasks such as following navigational instructions (Vogel and Jurafsky, 2010; Chen and Mooney, 2011; Tellex et al., 2011), software control (Branavan et al., 2009; Branavan et al., 2010), semantic parsing (Clarke et al., 2010; Liang et al., 2011) and learning to play games based on text (Branavan et al., 2011; Goldwasser and Roth, 2011).

In this paper, we present an approach to interpreting language instructions that describe *complex multipart tasks* by learning from pairs of instructions and behavioral traces containing a sequence of primitive actions that result in these instructions being properly followed. We do not assume a one-to-one mapping between instructions and primitive actions. Our approach uses three main subcomponents: (1) recognizing intentions from observed behavior using variations of Inverse Reinforcement Learning (IRL) methods; (2) translating instructions to task specifications using Semantic Parsing (SP) techniques; and (3) creating generalized task specifications to match user intentions using probabilistic Task Abstraction (TA) methods. We describe our system architecture and a learning scenario. We present preliminary results for a simplified version of our system that uses a unigram language model, minimal abstraction, and simple inverse reinforcement learning.

Early work on grounded language learning used features based on n-grams to represent the natural language input (Branavan et al., 2009; Vogel and Jurafsky, 2010). More recent methods have relied on a richer representation of linguistic data, such as syntactic dependency trees (Branavan et al., 2011; Goldwasser and Roth, 2011) and semantic templates (Tellex et al., 2011) to address the complexity of the natural language input. Our approach uses a flexible framework that allows us to incorporate various degrees of linguistic knowledge available at different stages in the learning process (e.g., from dependency relations to a full-fledged semantic model of the domain learned during training).

2 System Architecture

We represent tasks using the Object-oriented Markov Decision Process (OO-MDP) formalism (Diuk et al., 2008), an extension of Markov Decision Processes (MDPs) to explicitly capture relationships between objects. Specifically, OO-MDPs add a set of classes $\mathcal{C}$, each with a set of attributes $\mathcal{T}_\mathcal{C}$. Each OO-MDP state is defined by an unordered set of instantiated objects. In addition to these object definitions, an OO-MDP also defines a set of propositional functions that operate on objects. For instance, we might have a propositional function `toyIn(toy, room)` that operates on an object belonging to class "toy" and an object belonging to class "room," returning true if the specified "toy" object is in the specific "room" object. We extend OO-MDPs to include a set of *propositional function classes* ($\mathcal{F}$) associating propositional functions that describe similar properties. In the context of defining a task corresponding to a particular goal, an OO-MDP defines a subset of states $\beta \subset \mathcal{S}$ called *termination states* that end an action sequence and that need to be favored by the task's reward function.

Example Domain. To illustrate our approach, we present a simple domain called *Cleanup World*, a 2D grid world defined by various rooms that are connected by open doorways and can contain various objects (toys) that the agent can push around to different positions in the world. The Cleanup World domain can be represented as an OO-MDP with four object classes: agent, room, doorway, and toy, and a set of propositional functions that specify whether a toy is a specific shape (such as `isStar(toy)`), the color of a room (such as `isGreen(room)`), whether a toy is in a specific room (`toyIn(toy, room)`), and whether an agent is in a specific room (`agentIn(room)`). These functions belong to *shape*, *color*, *toy position* or *agent position* classes.

2.1 Interaction among IRL, SP and TA

The training data for the overall system is a set of pairs of verbal instructions and behavior. For example, one of these pairs could be the instruction *Push the star to the green room* with a demonstration of the task being accomplished in a specific environment containing various toys and rooms of different colors. We assume the availability of a set of features for each state represented using the OO-MDP propositional functions descibed previously. These features play an important role in defining the tasks to be learned. For example, a robot being taught to move furniture around would have information about whether or not it is currently carrying a piece of furniture, what piece of furniture it needs to be moving, which room it is currently in, which room contains each piece of furniture, etc. We present briefly the three components of our system (IRL, SP and TA) and how they interact with each other during learning.

Inverse Reinforcement Learning. Inverse Reinforcement Learning (Abbeel and Ng, 2004) addresses the task of learning a reward function from demonstrations of expert behavior and information about the state-transition function. Recently, more data-efficient IRL methods have been proposed, including the Maximum Likelihood Inverse Reinforcement Learning (Babeş-Vroman et al., 2011) or MLIRL approach, which our system builds on. Given even a small number of trajectories, MLIRL finds a weighting of the state features that (locally) maximizes the probability of these trajectories. In our system, these state features consist of one of the sets of propositional functions provided by the TA component. For a given task and a set of sets of state features, MLIRL evaluates the feature sets and returns to the TA component its assessment of the probabilities of the various sets.

Semantic Parsing. To address the problem of mapping instructions to semantic parses, we use a constraint-based grammar formalism, Lexicalized Well-Founded Grammar (LWFG), which has been shown to balance expressiveness with practical learnability results (Muresan and Rambow, 2007; Muresan, 2011). In LWFG, each string is associated with a syntactic-semantic representation, and the grammar rules have two types of constraints: one for semantic composition (Φ_c) and one for semantic interpretation (Φ_i). The semantic interpretation constraints, Φ_i, provide access to a semantic model (domain knowledge) during parsing. In the absence of a semantic model, however, the LWFG learnability result still holds. This fact is important if our agent is assumed to start with no knowledge of the task and domain. LWFG uses an ontology-based semantic representation, which is a logical form represented as a conjunction of atomic predicates. For example, the representation of the phrase *green room* is $\langle X_1.\mathit{is}{=}\mathit{green}, X.P_1 = X_1, X.\mathit{isa}{=}\mathit{room}\rangle$. The semantic representation specifies two concepts—`green` and `room`—connected through a property that can be uninstantiated in the absence of a semantic model, or instantiated via the Φ_i constraints to the property name (e.g, `color`) if such a model is present.

During the learning phase, the SP component, using an LWFG grammar that is learned offline, provides to TA the logical forms (i.e., the semantic parses, or the unlabeled dependency parses if no semantic model is given) for each verbal instruction. For example, for the instruction *Move the chair into the green room*, the semantic parser knows initially that *move* is a verb, *chair* and *room* are nouns, and *green* is an adjective. It also has grammar rules of the form S → Verb NP PP: Φ_{c1}, Φ_{i1},[1] but it has no knowledge of what these words mean (that is, to which concepts they map in the domain model). For this instruction, the LWFG parser returns the logical form:

$$\langle (X_1.\mathit{isa}{=}\mathit{move}, X_1.\mathit{Arg1}{=}\ X_2)_{\mathit{move}}, (X_2.\mathit{det}{=}\mathit{the})_{\mathit{the}}, (X_2.\mathit{isa}{=}\mathit{chair})_{\mathit{chair}}, (X_1.P_1 = X_3, P_2.\mathit{isa}{=}\mathit{into})_{\mathit{into}}, (X_3.\mathit{det}{=}\mathit{the})_{\mathit{the}}, (X_4.\mathit{isa}{=}\mathit{green}, X_3.P_2 = X_2)_{\mathit{green}}, (X_3.\mathit{isa}{=}\mathit{room})_{\mathit{room}}\rangle.$$

The subscripts for each atomic predicate indicate the word to which that predicate corresponds. This logical form corresponds to the simplified logical form `move(chair1, room1), P1(room1, green)`, where predicate P1 is uninstantiated. A key advantage of this framework is that the LWFG parser has access to the domain (semantic) model via Φ_i constraints. As a result, when TA provides feedback about domain-specific meanings (i.e., groundings), the parser can incorporate those mappings via the Φ_i constraints (e.g., *move* might map to the predicate `blockToRoom` with a certain probability).

Task Abstraction. The termination conditions for an OO-MDP task can be defined in terms of the propositional functions. For example, the Cleanup World domain might include a task that requires the agent to put a specific toy (t_1) in a specific room (r_1). In this case, the termination states would be defined by states that satisfy $\mathtt{toyIn}(t_1, r_1)$ and the reward function would be defined as $R_a(s, s') = \{1 : \mathtt{toyIn}(t_1^{s'}, r_1^{s'}); -1 : \mathtt{otherwise}\}$. However, such a task definition is overly specific and cannot be evaluated in a new environment that contains different objects. To remove this limitation, we define abstract task descriptions using *parametric lifted* reward and termination functions. A parametric lifted reward function is a first-order logic expression in which the propositional functions defining the reward can be selected as parameters. This representation allows much more general tasks to be defined; these tasks can be evaluated in any environment that contains the necessary object classes. For instance, the reward function for an abstract task that encourages an agent to take a toy of a certain shape to a room of a certain color (resulting in a reward of 1) would be represented as $R_a(s, s') = \{1 : \exists_{t^{s'} \in toy} \exists_{r^{s'} \in room} \mathtt{P1}(t) \wedge \mathtt{P2}(r) \wedge \mathtt{toyIn}(t, r); -1 : \mathtt{otherwise}\}$, where `P1` is a propositional function that operates on toy objects and `P2` is a propositional function that operates on room objects. An analogous definition can be made for termination conditions. Given the logical forms provided by SP, TA finds candidate tasks that might match each logical form, along with a set of possible *groundings* of those tasks. A grounding of an abstract task is the set of propositional functions to be applied to the specific objects in a given training instance. TA then passes these grounded propositional functions as the features to use in IRL. (If there are no candidate tasks, then it will pass all grounded propositional functions of the OO-MDP to IRL.) When IRL returns a reward function for these possible groundings and their likelihoods of representing the true reward function, TA determines whether any abstract tasks it has defined might match. If not, TA will either create a new abstract task that is consistent with the received reward functions or it will modify one of its existing definitions if doing so does not require significant changes. With IRL indicating the intended goal of a trace and with the abstract task indicating relevant parameters, TA can then inform SP of the task/domain specific meanings for the logical forms.

[1]For readability, we show here just the context-free backbone, without the augmented nonterminals or constraints.

A Learning from Scratch Scenario. Our system is trained using a set of sentence–trajectory pairs $((S_1, T_1), ..., (S_N, T_N))$. Initially, the system does not know what any of the words mean and there are no pre-existing abstract tasks. Let's assume that S_1 is *Push the star into the green room.*This sentence is first processed by the SP component, yielding the following logical forms: L_1 is $push(star1, room1), amod(room1, green)$ and L_2 is $push(star1), amod(room1, green)$, $into(star1, room1)$. These logical forms and their likelihoods are passed to the TA component, and TA induces incomplete abstract tasks, which define only the number and kinds of objects that are relevant to the corresponding reward function. TA can send to IRL a set of features involving these objects, together with T_1, the demonstration attached to S_1. This set of features might include: `agentTouchToy`(t_1), `toyIn`(t_1, r_1), `toyIn`(t_1, r_2), `agentIn`(r_1). IRL sends back a weighting of the features, and TA can select the subset of features that have the highest weights (e.g, (1.91, `toyIn`(t_1, r_1)), (1.12, `agentTouchToy`(t_1)), (0.80, `agentIn`(r_1)). Using information from SP and IRL, TA can now create a new abstract task, perhaps called `blockToRoom`, adjust the probabilities of the logical forms based on the relevant features obtained from IRL, and send these probabilities back to SP, enabling it to adjust its semantic model.

The entire system proceeds iteratively. While it is designed, not all features are fully implemented to be able to report experimental results. In the next section, we present a simplified version of our system and show preliminary results.

3 A Simplified Model and Experiments

In this section, we present a simplified version of our system with a unigram language model, inverse reinforcement learning and minimal abstraction. We call this version Model 0. The input to Model 0 is a set of verbal instructions paired with demonstrations of appropriate behavior. It uses an EM-style algorithm (Dempster et al., 1977) to estimate the probability distribution of words conditioned on reward functions (the parameters). With this information, when the system receives a new command, it can behave in a way that maximizes its reward given the posterior probabilities of the possible reward functions given the words.

Algorithm 1 shows our EM-style Model 0. For all possible reward–demonstration pairs, the E-step of EM estimates $z_{ji} = \Pr(R_j|(S_i, T_i))$, the probability that reward function R_j produced sentence-trajectory pair (S_i, T_i), This estimate is given by the equation below:

$$zji = \Pr(R_j|(S_i, T_i)) = \frac{\Pr(R_j)}{\Pr(S_i, T_i)} \Pr((S_i, T_i)|R_j)$$

$$= \frac{\Pr(R_j)}{\Pr(S_i, T_i)} \Pr(T_i|R_j) \prod_{w_k \in S_i} \Pr(w_k|R_j)$$

where S_i is the ith sentence, T_i is the trajectory demonstrated for verbal command S_i, and w_k is an element in the set of all possible words (vocabulary). If the reward functions R_j are known ahead of time, $\Pr(T_i|R_j)$ can be obtained directly by solving the MDP and estimating the probability of trajectory T_i under a Boltzmann policy with respect to R_j. If the R_js are not known, EM can estimate them by running IRL during the M-step (Babeş-Vroman et al., 2011).

The M-step in Algorithm 1 uses the current estimates of z_{ji} to further refine the probabilities $x_{kj} = \Pr(w_k|R_j)$:

$$x_{kj} = \Pr(w_k|R_j) = \frac{1}{X} \frac{\Sigma_{w_k \in S_i} \Pr(R_j|S_i) + \epsilon}{\Sigma_i N(S_i) z_{ji} + \epsilon}$$

where ϵ is a smoothing parameter, X is a normalizing factor and $N(S_i)$ is the number of words in sentence S_i.

To illustrate our Model 0 performance, we selected as training data six sentences for two tasks (three sentences for each task) from a dataset we have collected using Amazon Mechanical Turk for the Cleanup Domain. We show the training data in Figure 1. We obtained the reward function for each task using MLIRL, computed the $\Pr(T_i|R_j)$, then ran Algorithm 1 and obtained the parameters $\Pr(w_k|R_j)$. After this training process, we presented the agent with a new task. She is given the instruction S_N: *Go to green room.* and a starting state, somewhere in the same grid. Using parameters $\Pr(w_k|R_j)$, the agent can estimate:

Algorithm 1 EM-style Model 0

Input: Demonstrations $\{(S_1, T_1), ..., (S_N, T_N)\}$, number of reward functions J, size of vocabulary K.

Initialize: $x_{11}, \ldots, x_{JK}$, randomly.

repeat

E Step: Compute

$z_{ji} = \frac{\Pr(R_j)}{\Pr(S_i,T_i)} \Pr(T_i|R_j) \prod_{w_k \in S_i} x_{kj}$.

M step: Compute

$x_{kj} = \frac{1}{X} \frac{\Sigma_{w_k \in S_i} \Pr(R_j|S_i)+\epsilon}{\Sigma_i N(S_i) z_{ji}+\epsilon}$.

until target number of iterations completed.

$\Pr(S_N|R_1) = \prod_{w_k \in S_N} \Pr(w_k|R_1) = 8.6 \times 10^{-7}$, $\Pr(S_N|R_2) = \prod_{w_k \in S_N} \Pr(w_k|R_2) = 4.1 \times 10^{-4}$, and choose the optimal policy corresponding to reward R_2, thus successfully carrying out the task. Note that R_1 and R_2 corresponded to the two target tasks, but this mapping was determined by EM. We illustrate the limitation of the unigram model by telling the trained agent to *Go with the star to green*, (we label this sentence S'_N). Using the learned parameters, the agent computes the following estimates:
$\Pr(S'_N|R_1) = \prod_{w_k \in S'_N} \Pr(w_k|R_1) = 8.25 \times 10^{-7}$, $\Pr(S'_N|R_2) = \prod_{w_k \in S'_N} \Pr(w_k|R_2) = 2.10 \times 10^{-5}$. The agent wrongly chooses reward R_2 and goes to the green room instead of taking the star to the green room. The problem with the unigram model in this case is that it gives too much weight to word frequencies (in this case *go*) without taking into account what the words mean or how they are used in the context of the sentence. Using the system described in Section 2, we can address these problems and also move towards more complex scenarios.

4 Conclusions and Future Work

We have presented a three-component architecture for interpreting natural language instructions, where the learner has access to natural language input and demonstrations of appropriate behavior. Our future work includes fully implementing the system to be able to build abstract tasks from language information and feature relevance.

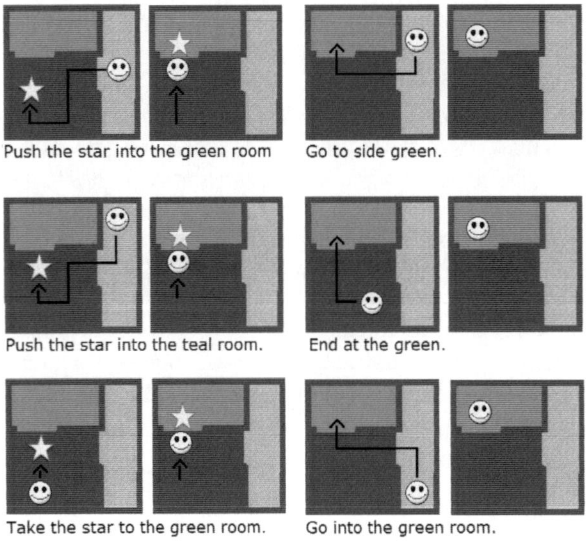

Figure 1: Training data for 2 tasks: Taking the star to the green room (left) and Going to the green room (right).

Acknowledgments

The authors acknowledge the support of the National Science Foundation (collaborative grant IIS-00006577 and IIS-1065195). The authors thank the anonymous reviewers for their feedback. Any opinions, findings, conclusions, or recommendations expressed in this paper are those of the authors, and do not necessarily reflect the views of the funding organization.

References

Pieter Abbeel and Andrew Ng. 2004. Apprenticeship learning via inverse reinforcement learning. In *Proceedings of the Twenty-First International Conference in Machine Learning (ICML 2004)*.

Yoav Atrzi and Luke Zettlemoyer. 2011. Bootstrapping semantic parsers for conversations. In *Proceedings of the 2011 Conference on Empirical Methods in Natural Language Processing*.

Monica Babeş-Vroman, Vukosi Marivate, Kaushik Subramanian, and Michael Littman. 2011. Apprenticeship learning about multiple intentions. In *Proceedings of the Twenty Eighth International Conference on Machine Learning (ICML 2011)*.

S. R. K. Branavan, Harr Chen, Luke S. Zettlemoyer, and Regina Barzilay. 2009. Reinforcement learning for mapping instructions to actions. In *Proceedings of the Joint Conference of the 47th Annual Meeting of the ACL and the 4th International Joint Conference on*

Natural Language Processing of the AFNLP: Volume 1 - Volume 1, ACL '09.

S. R. K. Branavan, Luke S. Zettlemoyer, and Regina Barzilay. 2010. Reading between the lines: Learning to map high-level instructions to commands. In *Association for Computational Linguistics (ACL 2010)*.

S.R.K. Branavan, David Silver, and Regina Barzilay. 2011. Learning to win by reading manuals in a monte-carlo framework. In *Association for Computational Linguistics (ACL 2011)*.

David L. Chen and Raymond J. Mooney. 2011. Learning to interpret natural language navigation instructions from observations. In *Proceedings of the 25th AAAI Conference on Artificial Intelligence (AAAI-2011).*, pages 859–865.

James Clarke, Dan Goldwasser, Ming-Wei Chang, and Dan Roth. 2010. Driving semantic parsing from the world's response. In *Proceedings of the Association for Computational Linguistics (ACL 2010)*.

A. P. Dempster, N. M. Laird, and D. B. Rubin. 1977. Maximum likelihood from incomplete data via the EM algorithm. *Journal of the Royal Statistical Society*, 39(1):1–38.

Carlos Diuk, Andre Cohen, and Michael Littman. 2008. An object-oriented representation for efficient reinforcement learning. In *Proceedings of the Twenty-Fifth International Conference on Machine Learning (ICML-08)*.

Dan Goldwasser and Dan Roth. 2011. Learning from natural instructions. In *Proceedings of the Twenty-Second International Joint Conference on Artificial Intelligence*.

Rohit J. Kate and Raymond J. Mooney. 2006. Using string-kernels for learning semantic parsers. In *Proceedings of the 21st International Conference on Computational Linguistics and the 44th annual meeting of the Association for Computational Linguistics*, ACL-44.

Percy Liang, Michael Jordan, and Dan Klein. 2011. Learning dependency-based compositional semantics. In *Association for Computational Linguistics (ACL 2011)*.

Wei Lu, Hwee Tou Ng, Wee Sun Lee, and Luke S. Zettlemoyer. 2008. A generative model for parsing natural language to meaning representations. In *Proceedings of the Conference on Empirical Methods in Natural Language Processing*, EMNLP '08.

Smaranda Muresan and Owen Rambow. 2007. Grammar approximation by representative sublanguage: A new model for language learning. In *Proceedings of ACL*.

Smaranda Muresan. 2011. Learning for deep language understanding. In *Proceedings of IJCAI-11*.

Stefanie Tellex, Thomas Kollar, Steven Dickerson, Matthew Walter, Ashis Gopal Banerjee, Seth Teller, and Nicholas Roy. 2011. Understanding natural language commands for robotic navigation and mobile manipulation. In *Proceedings of the Twenty-Fifth AAAI Conference on Articifical Intelligence*.

Adam Vogel and Dan Jurafsky. 2010. Learning to follow navigational directions. In *Association for Computational Linguistics (ACL 2010)*.

Yuk Wah Wong and Raymond Mooney. 2007. Learning synchronous grammars for semantic parsing with lambda calculus. In *Proceedings of the 45th Annual Meeting of the Association for Computational Linguistics (ACL-2007)*.

Luke S. Zettlemoyer and Michael Collins. 2005. Learning to map sentences to logical form: Structured classification with probabilistic categorial grammars. In *Proceedings of UAI-05*.

Luke Zettlemoyer and Michael Collins. 2009. Learning context-dependent mappings from sentences to logical form. In *Proceedings of the Association for Computational Linguistics (ACL'09)*.

Toward Learning Perceptually Grounded Word Meanings from Unaligned Parallel Data

Stefanie Tellex and **Pratiksha Thaker** and **Josh Joseph** and **Matthew R. Walter** and **Nicholas Roy**
MIT Computer Science and Artificial Intelligence Laboratory

Abstract

In order for robots to effectively understand natural language commands, they must be able to acquire a large vocabulary of meaning representations that can be mapped to perceptual features in the external world. Previous approaches to learning these *grounded* meaning representations require detailed annotations at training time. In this paper, we present an approach which is capable of jointly learning a policy for following natural language commands such as "Pick up the tire pallet," as well as a mapping between specific phrases in the language and aspects of the external world; for example the mapping between the words "the tire pallet" and a specific object in the environment. We assume the action policy takes a parametric form that factors based on the structure of the language, based on the G^3 framework and use stochastic gradient ascent to optimize policy parameters. Our preliminary evaluation demonstrates the effectiveness of the model on a corpus of "pick up" commands given to a robotic forklift by untrained users.

1 Introduction

In order for robots to robustly understand human language, they must have access to meaning representations capable of mapping between symbols in the language and aspects of the external world which are accessible via the robot's perception system. Previous approaches have represented word meanings as symbols in some specific symbolic language, either programmed by hand [Winograd, 1971, MacMahon et al., 2006] or learned [Matuszek et al., 2010, Chen and Mooney, 2011, Liang et al., 2011, Branavan et al., 2009]. Because word meanings are represented as symbols, rather than perceptually grounded features, the mapping between these symbols and the external world must still be defined. Furthermore, the uncertainty of the mapping between constituents in the language and aspects of the external world cannot be explicitly represented by the model.

Language grounding approaches, in contrast, map words in the language to *groundings* in the external world [Mavridis and Roy, 2006, Hsiao et al., 2008, Kollar et al., 2010, Tellex et al., 2011]. Groundings are the specific physical concept that is referred to by the language and can be objects (e.g., a truck or a door), places (e.g., a particular location in the world), paths (e.g., a trajectory through the environment), or events (e.g., a sequence of robot actions). This symbol grounding approach [Harnad, 1990] represents word meanings as *functions* which take as input a perceptual representation of a grounding and return whether it matches words in the language. Recent work has demonstrated how to learn grounded word meanings from a parallel corpus of natural language commands paired with groundings in the external world [Tellex et al., 2011]. However, learning model parameters required that the parallel corpus be augmented with additional annotations specifying the alignment between specific phrases in the language and corresponding groundings in the external world. Figure 1 shows an example command from the training set paired with these alignment annotations, represented as arrows pointing from each linguistic constituent to a corresponding grounding.

Our approach in this paper relaxes these annotation requirements and learns perceptually grounded word meanings from an *unaligned* parallel corpus that only provides supervision for the top-level action that corresponds to a natural language command. Our system takes as input a state/action space for the robot defining a space of possible groundings and available actions in the external world. In addition it requires a corpus of natural language commands paired with the correct action executed in the environment. For example, an entry in the corpus consists of a natural language command such as "Pick up the tire pallet" given to a robotic forklift, paired with an action sequence of the robot as drives to the tire pallet, inserts its forks, and raises it off the ground, drives to the truck, and sets it down.

To learn from an unaligned corpus, we derive a new training algorithm that combines the Generalized Grounding Graph (G^3) framework introduced by Tellex et al. [2011] with the policy gradient method described by Branavan et al. [2009]. We assume a specific parametric form for the action policy that is defined by the linguistic structure of the natural language command. The system learns a policy parameters that maximize expected reward using stochastic gradient ascent. By factoring the policy according to the structure of language, we can propagate the error signal to each term, allowing the system to infer groundings for each linguistic constituent even without direct supervision. We evaluate our model using a corpus of natural language commands collected from untrained users on the internet, commanding the robot to pick up objects or drive to locations in the environment. The evaluation demonstrates that the model is able to predict both robot actions and noun phrase groundings with high accuracy, despite having no direct supervision for noun phrase groundings.

Figure 1: Sample entry from an aligned corpus, where mappings between phrases in the language and groundings in the external world are explicitly specified as arrows. Learning the meaning of "the truck" and "the pallet" is challenging when alignment annotations are not known.

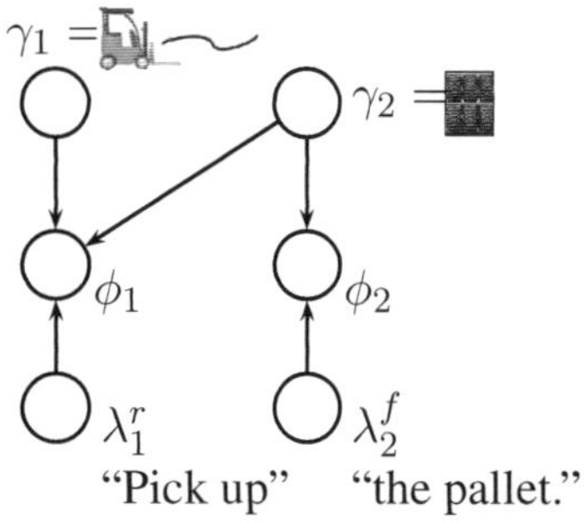

Figure 2: Grounding graph for "Pick up the tire pallet.

2 Background

We briefly review the G^3 framework, introduced by Tellex et al. [2011]. In order for a robot to understand natural language, it must be able to map between words in the language and corresponding groundings in the external world. The aim is to find the most probable groundings $\gamma_1 \dots \gamma_N$ given the language Λ and the robot's model of the environment M:

$$\underset{\gamma_1 \dots \gamma_N}{\operatorname{argmax}}\, p(\gamma_1 \dots \gamma_N | \Lambda, M) \tag{1}$$

M consists of the robot's location, the locations, geometries, and perceptual tags of objects, and available actions the robot can take. For brevity, we omit M from future equations in this section.

To learn this distribution, one standard approach is to factor it based on certain independence assumptions, then train models for each factor. Natural language has a well-known compositional, hierarchical argument structure [Jackendoff, 1983], and a promising approach is to exploit this structure in order to factor the model. However, if we define a directed model over these variables, we must assume a possibly arbitrary order to the conditional γ_i factors. For example, for a phrase such as "the tire pallet near the other skid," we could factorize in either of the following ways:

$$p(\gamma_{\text{tires}}, \gamma_{\text{skid}} | \Lambda) = p(\gamma_{\text{skid}} | \gamma_{\text{tires}}, \Lambda) \times p(\gamma_{\text{tires}} | \Lambda) \tag{2}$$

$$p(\gamma_{\text{tires}}, \gamma_{\text{skid}} | \Lambda) = p(\gamma_{\text{tires}} | \gamma_{\text{skid}}, \Lambda) \times p(\gamma_{\text{skid}} | \Lambda) \tag{3}$$

Depending on the order of factorization, we will need different conditional probability tables that correspond to the meanings of words in the language. To resolve this issue, another approach is to use Bayes' Rule to estimate the $p(\Lambda | \gamma_1 \dots \gamma_N)$, but this approach would require normalizing over all possible words in the language Λ. Another alternative is to use an undirected model, but this approach is intractable because it requires normalizing over all possible values of all γ_i variables in the model, including continuous attributes such as location and size.

To address these problems, the G^3 framework introduced a correspondence vector Φ to capture the dependency between $\gamma_1 \dots \gamma_N$ and Λ. Each entry in $\phi_i \in \Phi$ corresponds to whether linguistic constituent $\lambda_i \in \Lambda$ corresponds to grounding γ_i. We assume that $\gamma_1 \dots \gamma_N$ are independent of Λ *unless* Φ is known. Introducing Φ enables factorization according to the structure of language with local normalization at each factor over a space of just the two possible values for ϕ_i.

2.1 Inference

In order to use the G^3 framework for inference, we want to infer the groundings $\gamma_1 \dots \gamma_N$ that maximize the distribution

$$\underset{\gamma_1 \dots \gamma_N}{\operatorname{argmax}}\, p(\gamma_1 \dots \gamma_N | \Phi, \Lambda) \tag{4}$$

which is equivalent to maximizing the joint distribution of all groundings $\gamma_1 \dots \gamma_N$, Φ and Λ,

$$\underset{\gamma_1 \dots \gamma_N}{\operatorname{argmax}}\, p(\gamma_1 \dots \gamma_N, \Phi, \Lambda). \tag{5}$$

We assume that Λ and $\gamma_1 \dots \gamma_N$ are independent when Φ is not known, yielding:

$$\underset{\gamma_1 \dots \gamma_N}{\operatorname{argmax}}\, p(\Phi | \Lambda, \gamma_1 \dots \gamma_N) p(\Lambda) p(\gamma_1 \dots \gamma_N) \tag{6}$$

This independence assumption may seem unintuitive, but it is justified because the correspondence variable Φ breaks the dependency between Λ and $\gamma_1 \dots \gamma_N$. If we do not know whether $\gamma_1 \dots \gamma_N$ correspond to Λ, we assume that the language does not tell us anything about the groundings.

Finally, for simplicity, we assume that any object in the environment is equally likely to be referenced by the language, which amounts to a constant prior on $\gamma_1 \dots \gamma_N$. In the future, we plan to incorporate models of attention and salience into this prior. We ignore $p(\Lambda)$ since it does not depend on $\gamma_1 \dots \gamma_N$, leading to:

$$\underset{\gamma_1 \dots \gamma_N}{\operatorname{argmax}}\, p(\Phi | \Lambda, \gamma_1 \dots \gamma_N) \tag{7}$$

To compute the maximum value of the objective in Equation 7, the system performs beam search over $\gamma_1 \dots \gamma_N$, computing the probability of each assignment from Equation 7 to find the maximum probability assignment. Although we are using $p(\Phi | \Lambda, \gamma_1 \dots \gamma_N)$ as the objective function, Φ is fixed, and the $\gamma_1 \dots \gamma_N$ are unknown. This approach is valid because, given our independence assumptions, $p(\Phi | \Lambda, \gamma_1 \dots \gamma_N)$ corresponds to the joint distribution over all the variables given in Equation 5.

In order to perform beam search, we factor the model according to the hierarchical, compositional linguistic structure of the command:

$$p(\Phi | \Lambda, \gamma_1 \dots \gamma_N) = \prod_i p(\phi_i | \lambda_i, \gamma_{i_1} \dots \gamma_{i_k}) \tag{8}$$

This factorization can be represented graphically; we call the resulting graphical model the *grounding graph* for a natural language command. The directed model for the command "Pick up the pallet" appears in Figure 2. The λ variables correspond to language; the γ variables correspond to groundings in the external world, and the ϕ variables are $True$ if the groundings correspond to the language, and $False$ otherwise.

In the fully supervised case, we fit model parameters Θ using an aligned parallel corpus of labeled positive and negative examples for each linguistic constituent. The G^3 framework assumes a log-linear parametrization with feature functions f_j and feature weights θ_j:

$$p(\Phi|\Lambda, \gamma_1 \dots \gamma_N) = \tag{9}$$

$$\prod_i \frac{1}{Z} \exp(\sum_j \theta_j f_j(\phi_i, \lambda_i, \gamma_{i_1} \dots \gamma_{i_k})) \tag{10}$$

This function is convex and can be optimized with gradient-based methods [McCallum, 2002].

Features correspond to the degree to which each Γ correctly grounds λ_i. For a relation such as "on," a natural feature is whether the grounding corresponding to the head noun phrase is supported by the grounding corresponding to the argument noun phrases. However, the feature $supports(\gamma_i, \gamma_j)$ alone is not enough to enable the model to learn that "on" corresponds to $supports(\gamma_i, \gamma_j)$. Instead we need a feature that also takes into account the word "on:"

$$supports(\gamma_i, \gamma_j) \wedge (\text{"on"} \in \lambda_i) \tag{11}$$

3 Approach

Our goal is to learn model parameters for the G^3 framework from an unaligned corpus of natural language commands paired with robot actions. Previously, the system learned model parameters Θ using an aligned corpus in which values for all grounding variables are known at training time, and annotators provided both positive and negative examples for each factor. In this paper we describe how to relax this annotation requirement so that only the top-level action needs to be observed in order to train the model. It is easy and fast to collect data with these annotations, whereas annotating the values of all the variables, including negative examples is time-consuming and error prone. Once we know the model parameters we can use existing inference to find groundings corresponding to word meanings, as in Equation 4.

We are given a corpus of D training examples. Each example d consists of a natural language command Λ^d with an associated grounding graph with grounding variables Γ^d. Values for the grounding variables are not known, except for an observed value g_a^d for the top-level action random variable, γ_a^d. Finally, an example has an associated environmental context or semantic map M^d. Each environmental context will have a different set of objects and available actions for the robot. For example, one training example might contain a command given in an environment with a single tire pallet; another might contain a command given in an environment with two box pallets and a truck.

We define a sampling distribution to choose values for the Γ variables in the model using the G^3 framework with parameters Θ:

$$p(\Gamma^d|\Phi^d, \Lambda^d, M^d, \Theta) \tag{12}$$

Next, we define a reward function for choosing the correct grounding g_a for a training example:

$$r(\Gamma^d, g_a^d) = \begin{cases} 1 & \text{if } \gamma_a^d = g_a^d \\ -1 & \text{otherwise} \end{cases} \tag{13}$$

Here γ_a is a grounding variable for the top-level action corresponding to the command; it is one of the variables in the vector Γ. Our aim is to find model parameters that maximize expected reward when drawing values for Γ^d from $p(\Gamma^d|\Phi^d, \Lambda^d, M^d, \Theta)$ over the training set:

$$\underset{\Theta}{\operatorname{argmax}} \sum_d E_{p(\Gamma^d|\Phi^d,\Lambda^d,M^d,\Theta)} r(\Gamma^d, g_a^d) \tag{14}$$

Expanding the expectation we have:

$$\underset{\Theta}{\operatorname{argmax}} \sum_d \sum_{\Gamma}^{d} r(\Gamma^d, g_a^d) p(\Gamma^d|\Phi^d, \Lambda^d, M^d, \Theta) \tag{15}$$

We use stochastic gradient descent to find model parameters that maximize reward. First, we take the derivative of the expectation with respect to Θ. (We drop the d subscripts for brevity.)

$$\frac{\partial}{\partial \theta_k} E_{p(\Gamma|\Phi,\Lambda,M,\Theta)} r(\Gamma, g_a) = \sum_{\Gamma} r(\Gamma, g_a) \frac{\partial}{\partial \theta_k} p(\Gamma|\Phi, \Lambda, M, \Theta) \tag{16}$$

Focusing on the inner term, we expand it with Bayes' rule:

$$\frac{\partial}{\partial \theta_k} p(\Gamma|\Phi, \Lambda, M, \Theta) = \frac{\partial}{\partial \theta_k} \frac{p(\Phi|\Gamma, \Lambda, M, \Theta) p(\Gamma|\Lambda, M, \Theta)}{p(\Phi|\Lambda, M, \Theta)} \tag{17}$$

We assume the priors do not depend on Θ:

$$\frac{p(\Gamma|M)}{p(\Phi|\Lambda)} \frac{\partial}{\partial \theta_k} p(\Phi|\Gamma, \Lambda, M, \Theta) \tag{18}$$

For brevity, we compress Γ, Λ, and M in the variable X. Next, we take the partial derivative of the likelihood of Φ. First we assume each factor is independent.

$$\frac{\partial}{\partial \theta_k} p(\Phi|X, \Theta) = \frac{\partial}{\partial \theta_k} \prod_i p(\phi_i|X, \Theta) \tag{19}$$

$$= \prod_i p(\phi_i|X, \Theta) \times \left(\sum_j \frac{\frac{\partial}{\partial \theta_k} p(\phi_j|X, \Theta)}{p(\phi_j|X, \Theta)} \right) \tag{20}$$

Finally, we assume the distribution over ϕ_j takes a log-linear form with feature functions f_k and parameters θ_k, as in the G^3 framework.

$$\frac{\partial}{\partial \theta_k} p(\phi_j|X, \Theta) = p(\phi|X, \Theta) \times \left(f_k(\phi, X) - E_{p(\phi'|X,\Theta)} \left[f_k(\phi', X) \right] \right) \tag{21}$$

We substitute back into the overall expression for the partial derivative of the expectation:

$$\frac{\partial}{\partial \theta_k} E_{p(\Gamma|X,\Theta)} r(\Gamma, g_a) = E_{p(\Gamma|X,\Theta)} r(\Gamma, g_a) \times \left(\sum_j f_k(\phi_j, X) - E_{p(\phi'|X,\Theta)} \left[f_k(\phi', X) \right] \right) \tag{22}$$

Input:
Initial values for parameters, Θ^0.
Training dataset, D.
Number of iterations, T.
Step size, α.

$\Theta \leftarrow \Theta^0$
for $t \in T$ **do**
  for $d \in D$ **do**
    $\nabla_\Theta \leftarrow \frac{\partial}{\partial \theta_k} E_{p(\Gamma^d|\Phi^d,\Lambda^d,M^d,\Theta)} r(\Gamma^d, g_a^d)$
  end for
  $\Theta \leftarrow \Theta + \alpha \nabla_\Theta$
end for
Output: Estimate of parameters Θ

Figure 3: Training algorithm.

We approximate the expectation over Γ with highly probable bindings for the Γ and update the gradient incrementally for each example. The training algorithm is given in Figure 3.

4 Results

We present preliminary results for the learning algorithm using a corpus of natural language commands given to a robotic forklift. We collected a corpus of natural language commands paired with robot actions by showing annotators on Amazon Mechanical Turk a video of the robot executing an action and asking them to describe in words they would use to command an expert human operator to carry out the commands in the video. Frames from a video in our corpus, together with commands for that video appear in Figure 4. Since commands often spanned multiple parts of the video, we annotated the alignment between each top-level clause in the command and the robot's motion in the video. Our initial evaluation uses only commands from the corpus that contain the words "pick up" due to scaling issues when running on the entire corpus.

We report results using a random cost function as a baseline as well as the learned parameters on a training set and a held-out test set. Table 1 shows performance on a training set using small environments (with one or two other objects) and a test set of small and large environments (with up to six other objects).

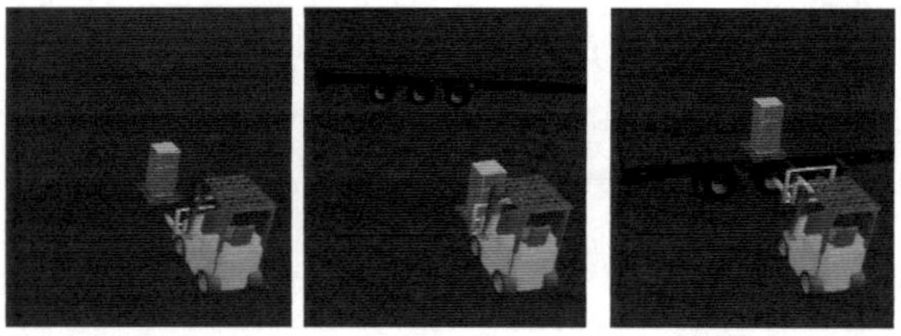

(a) t=0 (b) t=20 (c) t=30

```
Pick up pallet with refridgerator [sic] and place on truck to
the left.

A distance away you should see a rectangular box. Approach it
slowly and load it up onto your forklift. Slowly proceed to
back out and then make a sharp turn and approach the truck.
Raise your forklift and drop the rectangular box on the back of
the truck.

Go to the pallet with the refrigerator on it and pick it
up. Move the pallet to the truck trailer. Place the pallet on
the trailer.

Pick up the pallet with the refrigerator and place it on
the trailer.
```

(d) Commands

Figure 4: Frames from a video in our dataset, paired with natural language commands.

	% Correct	
	Actions	Concrete Noun Phrases
Before Training	31%	61%
After Training	100%	92%

(a) Training (small environments)

	% Correct	
	Actions	Concrete Noun Phrases
Before Training	3%	26%
After Training	84%	77%

(b) Testing (small and large environments)

Table 1: Results on the training set and test set.

As expected, on the training set the system learns a good policy, since it is directly rewarded for acting correctly. Because the environments are small, the chance of correctly grounding concrete noun phrases with a random cost function is high. However after training performance at grounding noun phrases increases to 92% even though the system had no access to alignment annotations for noun phrases at training time; it only observes reward based on whether it has acted correctly.

Next, we report performance on a test set to assess generalization to novel commands given in novel environments. Since the test set includes larger environments with up to six objects, baseline performance is lower. However the trained system is able to achieve high performance at both inferring correct actions as well as correct object groundings, despite having no access to a reward signal of any kind during inference. This result shows the system has learned general word meanings that apply in novel contexts not seen at training time.

5 Related Work

Beginning with SHRDLU [Winograd, 1971], many systems have exploited the compositional structure of language to statically generate a plan corresponding to a natural language command [Hsiao et al., 2008, MacMahon et al., 2006, Skubic et al., 2004, Dzifcak et al., 2009]. Our work moves beyond this framework by defining a probabilistic graphical model according to the structure of the natural language command, inducing a distribution over plans and groundings.

Models that learned word meanings [Tellex et al., 2011, Kollar et al., 2010] require detailed alignment annotations between constituents in the language and objects, places, paths, or events in the external world. Previous approaches capable of learning from unaligned data [Vogel and Jurafsky, 2010, Branavan et al., 2009] used sequential models that could not capture the hierarchical structure of language. Matuszek et al. [2010], Liang et al. [2011] and Chen and Mooney [2011] describe models that learn compositional semantics, but word meanings are symbolic structures rather than patterns of features in the external world.

There has been a variety of work in transferring action policies between a human and a robot. In imitation learning, the goal is to create a system that can watch a teacher perform an action, and then reproduce that action [Kruger et al., 2007, Chernova and Veloso, 2009, Schaal et al., 2003, Ekvall and Kragic, 2008]. Rybski et al. [2007] developed an imitation learning system that learns from a combination of imitation of the human teacher, as well as natural language input. Our work differs in that the system must infer an action from the natural language commands, rather than from watching the teacher perform an action. The system is trained off-line, and the task of the robot is to respond on-line to the natural language command.

6 Conclusion

In this paper we described an approach for learning perceptually grounded word meanings from an unaligned parallel corpus of language paired with robot actions. The training algorithm jointly infers policies that correspond to natural language commands as well as alignments between noun phrases in the command and groundings in the external world. In addition, our approach learns grounded word meanings or distributions corresponding to words in the language, that the system can use to follow novel commands that it may have never encountered during training. We presented a preliminary evaluation on a small corpus, demonstrating that the system is able to infer meanings for concrete noun phrases despite having no direct supervision for these values.

There are many directions for improvement. We plan to train our system using a large dataset of language paired with robot actions in more complex environments, and on more than one robotic platform. Our approach points the way towards a framework that can learn a large vocabulary of general grounded word meanings, enabling systems that flexibly respond to a wide variety of natural language commands given by untrained users.

References

S. R. K. Branavan, H. Chen, L. S. Zettlemoyer, and R. Barzilay. Reinforcement learning for mapping instructions to actions. In *Proceedings of ACL*, page 82–90, 2009.

D. L. Chen and R. J. Mooney. Learning to interpret natural language navigation instructions from observations. In *Proc. AAAI*, 2011.

S. Chernova and M. Veloso. Interactive policy learning through confidence-based autonomy. *JAIR*, 34 (1):1–25, 2009.

J. Dzifcak, M. Scheutz, C. Baral, and P. Schermerhorn. What to do and how to do it: Translating natural language directives into temporal and dynamic logic representation for goal management and action execution. In *Proc. IEEE Int'l Conf. on Robotics and Automation (ICRA)*, pages 4163–4168, 2009.

S. Ekvall and D. Kragic. Robot learning from demonstration: a task-level planning approach. *International Journal of Advanced Robotic Systems*, 5(3), 2008.

S. Harnad. The symbol grounding problem. *Physica D*, 43:335–346, 1990.

K. Hsiao, S. Tellex, S. Vosoughi, R. Kubat, and D. Roy. Object schemas for grounding language in a responsive robot. *Connection Science*, 20(4): 253–276, 2008.

R. S. Jackendoff. *Semantics and Cognition*, pages 161–187. MIT Press, 1983.

T. Kollar, S. Tellex, D. Roy, and N. Roy. Toward understanding natural language directions. In *Proc. ACM/IEEE Int'l Conf. on Human-Robot Interaction (HRI)*, pages 259–266, 2010.

V. Kruger, D. Kragic, A. Ude, and C. Geib. The meaning of action: A review on action recognition and mapping. *Advanced Robotics*, 21(13), 2007.

P. Liang, M. I. Jordan, and D. Klein. Learning dependency-based compositional semantics. In *Proc. Association for Computational Linguistics (ACL)*, 2011.

M. MacMahon, B. Stankiewicz, and B. Kuipers. Walk the talk: Connecting language, knowledge, and action in route instructions. In *Proc. Nat'l Conf. on Artificial Intelligence (AAAI)*, pages 1475–1482, 2006.

C. Matuszek, D. Fox, and K. Koscher. Following directions using statistical machine translation. In *Proc. ACM/IEEE Int'l Conf. on Human-Robot Interaction (HRI)*, pages 251–258, 2010.

N. Mavridis and D. Roy. Grounded situation models for robots: Where words and percepts meet. In *2006 IEEE/RSJ International Conference on Intelligent Robots and Systems*, pages 4690–4697. IEEE, Oct. 2006. ISBN 1-4244-0258-1.

A. K. McCallum. MALLET: A machine learning for language toolkit. http://mallet.cs.umass.edu, 2002.

P. Rybski, K. Yoon, J. Stolarz, and M. Veloso. Interactive robot task training through dialog and demonstration. In *Proceedings of HRI*, page 56. ACM, 2007.

S. Schaal, A. Ijspeert, and A. Billard. Computational approaches to motor learning by imitation. *Phil. Trans. R. Soc. Lond. B*, (358), 2003.

M. Skubic, D. Perzanowski, S. Blisard, A. Schultz, W. Adams, M. Bugajska, and D. Brock. Spatial language for human-robot dialogs. *IEEE Trans. on Systems, Man, and Cybernetics, Part C: Applications and Reviews*, 34(2):154–167, 2004. ISSN 1094-6977.

S. Tellex, T. Kollar, S. Dickerson, M. Walter, A. Banerjee, S. Teller, and N. Roy. Understanding natural language commands for robotic navigation and mobile manipulation. In *Proc. AAAI*, 2011.

A. Vogel and D. Jurafsky. Learning to follow navigational directions. In *Proc. Association for Computational Linguistics (ACL)*, pages 806–814, 2010.

T. Winograd. *Procedures as a Representation for Data in a Computer Program for Understanding Natural Language*. PhD thesis, Massachusetts Institute of Technology, 1971. Ph.D. thesis.

Author Index